PRAISE FOR *EXIT~SKY*

"Warren Woessner's poetry offers the kind of respite we long for on long winter nights, in the fiercest weather, or in the cradle of deep loss. He sees the beauty of the ordinary sky or bird or ruffle of water and lifts it into its rightful place, radiating beauty in smallness and giving the reader a moment to pause and examine the time we have all spent on earth without being awake enough to miss what is already disappearing. These are not celebrations of mourning, rather Woessner gives us the context to examine our lives, to measure ourselves in the vanishing world. He is at the height of his poetic powers here, and we need to share this book with friends and loved ones-it's that good."

— JONIS AGEE, author of *The Bones of Paradise*

"Warren Woessner's laconic poems, packed with silences, possess so much power in their observations of the natural world, one begins to feel beneath their surfaces, something beginning to move."

—JUSTEN AHREN, Martha's Vineyard Poet Laureate and author of *A Machine For Remembering*

BOOKS BY WARREN WOESSNER

Exit - Sky, Holy Cow! Press (2019)

Clear All the Rest of the Way, Backwaters Press (2008)

Our Hawk, Toothpaste, Coffee House Press (2005)

Chemistry, Pudding House (2002)

Iris Rising, BkMk-UM-KC Press (1998)

Clear to Chukchi, Poetry Harbor Press (1995)

Storm Lines, New River Press (1987)

No Hiding Place, Spoon River Press (1979)

Landing, Ithaca House (1973)

The Forest and the Trees, Quixote Press (1968)

EXIT ~ SKY

Poems by

WARREN
WOESSNER

Holy Cow! Press
Duluth, Minnesota
2019

Author photograph by Iris C. Freeman.
Cover photograph, "Atmospheric-Black Skimmers,"
by Lanny McDowell.
Book and cover design by Anton Khodakovsky.

Printed and bound in the United States.
First printing, Fall, 2019
ISBN 978-1513645605

10 9 8 7 6 5 4 3 2 1

Holy Cow! Press projects are funded in part by grant awards from the
Ben and Jeanne Overman Charitable Trust, the Elmer L. and Eleanor
J. Andersen Foundation, the Lenfestey Family Foundation, and by gifts
from generous individual donors.

Holy Cow! Press books are distributed to the trade by Consortium
Book Sales & Distribution, c/o Ingram Publisher Services, Inc.,
210 American Drive, Jackson, TN 38301.

For inquiries, please write to: HOLY COW! PRESS,
Post Office Box 3170, Mount Royal Station, Duluth, MN 55803.
Visit *www.holycowpress.org*

ACKNOWLEDGEMENTS

Grateful acknowledgement is made to the editors of the following publications in which some of the poems in this volume have been previously published.

5 AM: "It Might as Well Be Spring," "March Cleanup," "Closing Time," "Navigator"

Abraxas: "Mother at 85," "One Page," "McDonalds: Further Excavations at a New Site," "Before Ice Over," "Office Visit"

Big Hammer: "7th Decade," "Industrial Park"

Big Scream: "Picking Wild Blueberries," "Keepsakes," "Canoes in January," "Cloud Window," "Moving"

Caprice: "End of a Hot Day"

Hearse: "All Night Summer Storms"

Iconoclast: "Prairie Grass – February"

Image: "Poem"

Kingfisher: "Barred Owl"

The Lake Street Review: "The King of New Jersey," "Entrance"

Legal Studies Forum: "After Marin-An"

Literary Accents: "Cloud Window"

Vineyard Gazette: "The Catch," "Farm House," "Before Ice Over," "Strong Finish," "Sugar Snap Rabbit," "Gay Head Light"

Midwest Quarterly: "The Chair," "Holdout"

Mimeo: "Flotsam"

Minnesota Binding: "Heron on Rock-Snow"

Minotaur: "Terminal Velocity"

Modine Gunch: "Another Forest"

On the Seawall (Online): "Collision Course"

Poetry Motel: "How to Protect Against Sharks"

Raven's Perch (Online): "Volcanes de Colima," "Strong Finish," "Exit - Sky," "Roost"

Shepherd Express (Online): "Sugar Snap Rabbit"

South Dakota Review: "Good-By Wisconsin"

Street Value: "Thrift Shop"

Tampa Review: "Halloween"

UT Poetry Review: "Garbage Collection – South Philly," "Winter News"

ANTHOLOGIES:

Eating the Pure Light, Homage to Thomas McGrath (The Backwaters Press): "One Page"

A Legal Studies Forum Poetry Anthology (Legal Studies Forum): "Before Ice Over," "Open House," "Strong Finish"

Except for Love: New England Poets Inspired by Donald Hall (Encircle Pubs., 2019): "Farm House," "Before Ice Over," "March Clean-Up"

for

IRIS C. FREEMAN

CONTENTS

STRONG FINISH

TAKING FLIGHT

ENTRANCE

Pause at a rise
in the muddy trail.
No sound.
The new leaves
don't move.

Don't look.
See.
Don't listen.
Hear.

The woods flow
like warm rain
into old snow.
Breathe in
what you need.

PICKING WILD BLUEBERRIES

I know I must finish
before the pebble rattles
start in the trees.

There is more fruit
on the branches closest
to the clearing
because there is less shelter
for the birds.

I see gray and white ones
waiting for me to finish:
"Wisaakegjak." "Whiskey Jacks,"
say the French who buy our pemmican.
Some day you will call them "Canada Jays."

HOLDOUT

After the embers from the fire die
to a glowing pile, a last blade of flame
might snap up, for a minute or two, light
the dark room again.

So too the scrawny, bent maple
lost all summer by the creek
hangs on to its leaves
after days of cold rain.

Other leaves down, already compost.
Maple still flares pure gold
warms up one corner
of this dim, abbreviated day.

This stanza should be cheery
or at least hopeful, but it's not.
Those leaves will fall.
It's going to snow,

and you'll sit there
and watch the dying coals
make faces at you
until they go out.

ROOST

At dusk, a few crows circle
over the river. Others join them
and the soaring spiral
expands, like they are holding
a place in the sky.

They are like words
in search of poems
no one wants to write.

Then the leader heads
straight for the roost
and the spiral unwinds,
and the black book goes
back on the shelf
for the night, unread.

THRIFT SHOP

I'm going through the rack
of men's trousers
in the musty basement
alongside a tall, skinny guy
I don't want to look at
twice, but he starts to talk:
"Everything in here's a 42
or XX large. Some fat guy
musta died last week."

Just then, I find a nice pair
of corduroys – 36 waist
too long, but I have a friend
who can hem.
I don't try them on, just pay
the $3 and get out.
I know I won't care who
I'm wearing on the white carpet
of snow already unrolling
under all those cold stars.

CLOSING TIME

Last night, smoke,
steak and wine.
Up late – endless talk
about right women
and wrong women

This morning it's clear
and cold. You cover
the pontoon boat
while I watch warblers
blow away over the pond
like yellow leaves.

In my hand, any one
of them would be warmer
than that bottle
left out by the empty chairs
and the dead fire.
It's half-full, but no one
is in a hurry to take it
into the house.

WINTER NEWS

Should I bring you flowers –
winter bouquets,
porcelain petals
glazed with ice?

You have a warm place,
a pink rug,
a rocking chair.

Below us, tires scream,
people hurry by, wrapped tight
in their destinations.
All over, snow blowing,
breaking the rooftops
into impossible black and white.

ALL NIGHT SUMMER STORMS

Chase each other
like huge black cats,
electric paws
feeling for church steeples,
clawing lonely trees.

You too, woman
asleep beside me, know
how they prowl all night
and disappear come morning.

END OF A HOT DAY

At 3 a.m. the dogs
start barking.

Birds lower their wings,
close their beaks.

The apartment still roars
with the artillery of air conditioners
but the fronts have shifted.

I think of you
frozen on our bed,
dreams condensing
gentle and distant as tomorrow's clouds.

ANOTHER FOREST

Your feet feel down
the sandy paths
where cut-up moonlight seeps
through unpruned branches.
Stop, you are surrounded
by sounds not from wind
or leaves. Worlds
of insects crackle
with unsteady life.
Fox, rabbit, snake, owl
all going their ways.

BARRED OWL

Swoops into the crest
of the big cottonwood
by the creek,
but can't escape the mob
of crows at his heels.
So he sits tight
like a fat banker –
tongue-tied, twisting
to watch all ways at once
while the James Gang
tugs his watch chain,
turns his pockets inside out.

HERON ON ROCK — SNOW

Young egret poised
on rip-rap river bank
under concrete pylons
of freeway bridge.
Too far north
in November.
Insects, lizards
and frogs – food
freezing over
almost as I watch,
wish, for once,
for flight.

OPEN HOUSE

In November, the forest feels
downhearted.
Someone left all the doors
and windows open!

Fall is in foreclosure:
the heat has been turned off,
the light evicted, leaves fallen
like fading "for sale" signs.

Some tenants won't move.
Juncos and sparrows
pick off weed seeds.
One robin brightens a hackberry.

I sit alone on a stone bench.
The old hermit, Han Shan,
sits down with me.
We scribble poems on dead leaves.

BEFORE ICE OVER

At dusk, one by one,
hundreds of gulls fall
out of the leaden sky
onto the lake, already
beginning to close
its lid for winter.

We call them
by their names,
recognize bill color,
molt, age, species –
see everything
but living beings –

finding their spots
for the night, calling out
to kin, to neighbors.
Afloat on freezing waves,
they turn together
into the north wind.

While, on shore, wrapped
in down coats, hats and gloves,
we strain to see
every last one
in the failing light, like
it was some miracle.

CANOES IN JANUARY

Tipped over, summer and fall
spilled out, winter
moved into aluminum
long houses
for Lakota ghosts.
Hulls still point
at the lake
like compass needles
point at true loss.

PRAIRIE GRASS — FEBRUARY

Almost touching the snow banks,
the thin stalks are bent down
like old women, walking home
from a country market, empty
early. They are holding
just a handful of seeds –
shopping baskets full of wind.

LOOK OUT

Millions of squirrel tracks in the snow
under empty nut trees.
Blue Jays argue.
"Three feet above your head –
the spirits!"

POEM FOR NEW PAPER

I felt the ground turn its back
when we last walked; the sky
no more then covered us. . .
    I can't
       tune you to my world, now
       everything sounds the same
(Only the wind frets
       new chords.)
and even the trees can't keep their leaves
through these days of changing.

INDUSTRIAL PARK

Not a park but not industrial either.
A mile of new road with nice curbs
carved into the prairie just outside
an ambitious little village
without fast food or a stoplight.

Now, just one rusty rail spur
to drop off ag chemicals
for the soybean fields that stop
just short of where all
those good-paying jobs

were penciled in, decades ago,
it seems, today, where I sit
in the car, windows down.
Western Meadowlark's bubbly call
to the east, Eastern Meadowlark's
slide whistle to the west.

In the muddy furrows, Vesper Sparrows
and larks contest. A Harrier
tips by, looking for distracted voles.
I'm eating a day-old sandwich
and drinking a week-old Coke,
content to watch the land fill up
with spring at least once again.

MARCH CLEAN-UP

Today the trees
have an early spring wind
in their hair,
combing out the tangles
with a stiff brush,
shushing the little ones –
making them bow down
then stand up straight,
and hold out fresh clean hands
for me to admire.

I find an elder long dead
but still standing.
Years of woodpecker
and insect holes
perforate frail cellulose bones.
I should let nature
take its course,
but being in that course,
I give it one good push,
watch it crash
from the air-making world
back to making earth.

FARM HOUSE

The first night in the country
I woke in the dark dark –
put my hand in front of my face
and couldn't tell my hand
was there.

Got a night light the next day.
Just one Christmas tree bulb
but so bright in the bathroom
I had to close the door to sleep.

This year we're back
and it's burned out.
I turn off the bedroom lamp
afraid to admit I'm afraid
of the dark we paid so much for.

But light pours through the blinds.
It's from a half moon,
unbreakable mirror,
sending sunlight
to this half of the earth
for free..

SUGAR SNAP RABBIT

Great cook, descendent
of green grocers, pickle
makers and bakers
in the markets of Poland
and Romania.
Now poised for the first
harvest from the herb garden
set in rotten stone and old logs
just beyond the kitchen window:

wiggy clumps of chives,
pushy mint, sour sorrel,
pungent oregano –
you love them all,
even the sappy plastic
lawn bunnies, snuggled
all winter under the snow,
emerging in late April,
indestructible,
under a tarragon umbrella.

By mid-May the snowbirds
will return to black earth –
plant delicate parsley,
limpid basil, rosemary,
a fake evergreen
that can't bluff February.

But it's spring,
and with sheers you go out
like a barber whose customers
hold still for the short cut
and keep coming back with more.

For Iris Freeman

HALLOWEVE

The road to the back parking lot
was blocked, so I parked and walked
in to a reserved picnic area
where a Ground Dove was found
three days ago – might stick around.

Then I pass a fake tombstone
for Elena Anderson 1819-1839,
then ghost sheets and a half-skeleton
hung from a branch, a tattered angel
and a monster black cat, complete
with battery-powered flashing red eyes.

It's the "Street of Screams,"
one of those haunted trails for kids
that I bet gets pretty scary at night
with flashlights and a sound track.

It's not dark yet, but the light
is failing. I reach the lot
but it's empty – no birds –
just one other guy in a black hoody
and muddy jeans, walking
along the curb slowly, like I do now.

I see him sit on an empty picnic table
and stare, like he's waiting
for company. I walk over,
"Peaceful, isn't it?" I ask. "Yes
it is," he says, not looking up.
Then I see he doesn't have binoculars.
Then I see he doesn't have eyes.

GOOD-BY WISCONSIN

1.
The voices have always been speaking:
a faint murmur crossing the Appalachians,
spreading over the prairie, pure
creamery butter arriving
like the gentle wash from an alleged tidal wave
here in Wisconsin.
Our poets fight to ignore them, get high,
and fly mission after mission deep into enemy territory.

2.
The Senate Bar has the loneliest jukebox around,
where country boys pitch pennies and remember Roy Acuff.
In Sun Prairie, the Auto Daredevils make their cars roll over
like dogs and push good luck medals, priests
ministering to the faithful, who still believe in miracles.
All over God's Country, men risk their lives
to speak on family planning. Our poets write
and write, getting it down.
No one believes a word.

3.
Wisconsin is a state without wonders, where lakes
are manufactured overnight,
and hills are called mountains.
The people have large families, play baseball,
and drink beer. They've learned all they need
to know: Chicago's the capitol, Iraq's
farther even than Omaha.
Small towns float, aimlessly, like life rafts
slowly losing air. The survivors have run out of songs.

4.
Our poets hear the voices and slowly their heads begin to turn.
We look around and they are gone –
like children who play with imaginary friends,
and one day stray from the picnic.

For David Hilton

STRONG
FINISH

COLLISION COURSE

I was driving home from Boy Scout Camp –
my first job – praise accepted, farewells said –
still some summer left – going eighty
down the Alloway Road.

Then the uniform I had hung
in the back caught the air, whipped around,
half out the window. I reached
back to grab it, eyes off the road
just two seconds, looked back

at a row of big trees at the edge
of the asphalt two-lane
I was about to leave – pulled
the wheel left – not hard enough

to skid, and the passenger side
hit a tree just behind the back door
and crushed the fender
like it was a beer can.
But I was back on the road, intact
heading straight for home.

Don't think I didn't thank
my guardian angel, animal instinct
or whoever wired the warning signal
into my neurons years before GPS,
back-up cameras and automatic
highway spacing control.

Thirty years later, the warning light
comes back on – this time she's 29,
beautiful, smart with an edge, intrigued—
of course – by everything I do or say.
She wants oh wants to be my muse.

But she's not my guardian angel –
has no intention of helping me get home
to my life in one piece.
Again, I'm going eighty
down that narrow road
In a much nicer car. I know

she's in the back seat already
and I'll turn my head. I'll reach
for her and the trees will be right there,
have been waiting with all the time
I have left in the world.

MOVING

I hear the tugs calling
each other on the Hudson
awash with moonlight
which washes over me as well –
adrift in the city.
Pigeon leader coos orders
and I go with him
off a ragged roof edge.
Sometimes I sleep with the bums,
warmed by their bottles,
warming cement. Other times
with soft women under coverlets
made from the feathers
of endangered species.
Adrift in the city
without a name.

NEW YEAR'S EVE

5 p.m., corner booth,
Oak Bar, Plaza Hotel,
New York City, Center
of the World of all
that matters.

Where a Belvedere martini,
up with a twist, contemplates you
like a languid gold fish
in a clear garden pool,
or a suspended tear

that you can take back inside,
like that first full breath,
in case you need it,
as the world gets ready
to start over again again.

ONE PAGE

October 11, 2001

Walking east on Murray Street
four blocks north of Ground Zero
in a sour, smoky wind,
I watch workers hose off windows.
"God Bless America" is smeared
on the hood of a smashed car
abandoned in a tiny lot
by a closed bar.

Then I see some sheets of paper
caught under a chain link fence –
not just deli wrappers or handbills –
but book pages, loose as dead leaves.
I pick one up. It's from the end
of a law book. The edges are gone,
not burned, but sheared,
punched out of the volume
with every other page by a wave
of awful force.

It's partly coated
with a gray crust from the walls
and shelves that held it up
in a library in the sky, gone now
like the doomed volumes
of Alexandria or Atlantis.

So I stand there in the cold
holding a relic as delicate
as any parchment or papyrus scroll.
I want to be its curator –
clean it, make repairs,
find its mates and bind them all
into a book again.

But I can't, so I just open my hand
and it is gone, turning, spinning up
lost in one gritty gust.

MCDONALDS: FURTHER EXCAVATIONS AT A NEW SITE

When food became scarce, many ritual shrines
were constructed where the followers of meat
might be admitted after lengthy ordeal.
Costly, indestructible materials were used:
plastics, tile, and steel that would not rust.
The chosen assembled in pews
beneath friezes and statues of the minor gods.
Priestesses cooked the symbolic foods
with electric fire. So important were these temples,
we surmise, that when food became extinct
the faithful still came here, until the end,
to worship at the feet of their "Hamburger" god.

THE KING OF NEW JERSEY

There must be one.
His subjects line up in rows
of housing. When there's work
they're always on the job.
New factories rise from dead ones
and now they're called plants.
The skeletons of the oldest still stand
with the petrified grace of ruined castles –
gutted, windows shot out,
but the revolution failed.

CLOUD WINDOW

Blocks from here, towers
scrape the sky.
In this warehouse,
workers who scrape to get by,
strain to see the sky.
One window tipped open
catches clouds,
keeps them outside.

AFTER MARIN-AN

Woke at 5 a.m. to the steady sigh
of tires on the bridge.
So many starting the day so soon.
"Cars driving men to work."

There is different sigh I've heard
while sitting in a White Pine grove –
light breeze slowed
by soft green needles.

EXIT - SKY

Young black
Jack Pine
explodes into crows
that, leaving, leave
next to nothing
behind.

STRONG FINISH

I hear you are
"mostly asleep now,"
"slipping away," but I don't see
a hospice bed, surrounded
by flowers and stilled grandchildren.

I remember the gull
I saw yesterday – full adult –
bright white in low sun,
beating into a bitter winter wind
over rough water.

Then, for its own reasons,
veering down and away
to some remembered shelter
for the night.

All that strength, just gone.
Empty sky.
Short day, suddenly
out of light.

IT MIGHT AS WELL BE SPRING

You didn't make it
to the first day of spring.
My father did, barely,
and so did David. But,
like the song says,
"It might as well be spring."

The grocery store tulips
on the table are limp,
but rain is beating down
the mountains of dirty snow
in big box parking lots,
and the Cancer Society ladies
are out in force, selling daffodils

picked far south of here,
of the country graveyard
you had time to choose –
no flowers, but adorned again
with the first Red-winged Blackbirds.

KEEPSAKES

Every few years, Dad
would bring out the vials
of perfume he'd mixed up
with Uncle Al, who later sold
the business Dad didn't help start
to IFF (look it up).

But Dad stayed at DuPont –
"Better Things for Better Living
Through Chemistry" –
where he said he had a job
he could count on –
and he could, up until
he died of cancer,

and Mom moved us
across town
to a smaller house.
It wasn't far, but those vials
Didn't make the trip.

DIAMONDS ARE FOREVER

After your father died, we found dozens of envelopes
folded from stiff waxy paper.
Each held tiny diamonds, not chips
or fragments, but each one cut,
some small as snowflakes
you couldn't melt on your tongue
or anywhere else, except maybe
in the fires of hell

where we hoped he'd miss
his timid, worn-out wife,
his hopeless son, who ate himself
to death after his wife finally left.
She died alone, except for the pills
she didn't have time to swallow.

At best, I'd say he was not a delicate man –
but all his life proud of his fingers:
Slavic-thick but sensitive and steady
enough to guide the smallest baguette
into its proper place, and make it stay.

"Mo The Jeweler": in his prime, no more
than a footnote mobster, proud
of his custom shirts, his aging Caddy,
kissing the owner after he ordered for us
from his corner table at Lorenzo's,
a faded failing "Family" joint,
once maybe the Umberto's Clam House
of Hialeah, Florida.

Two days later, he was in the ground,
next to a space for Mae, more than ready
to join him on that cruise ship
in the sky. No ashes to scatter
any place special.

But home up north again,
I'm sorry I can't wait
for a snow-shower
in the sun, then open
just one folder in the wind –
freeing the diamonds he worked so hard
to buy, to guard, to set just so.

THE CATCH

Today, I can't write
about having a second cup
of coffee or how
I interrupted my wife's dreams

to retrieve the covers,
or even how that nasty Blue
clipped my line
and vanished beneath the waves
off Devil's Bridge.

No, I must recall racing
across the choppy Sound
for port, our power cat
listing as the port hull

filled with water, getting in
from somewhere, and the bilge pump
no more use than coffee can bailing.

Then the captain, our jovial friend,
is our stern God, getting us
into life jackets, grouping us
to counteract the tilt, radioing
the Coast Guard with urgency

well short of panic, we hoped,
watching the breakwaters
get closer and closer as we came in
full throttle, past the "No Wake" signs.

Fishers gawked from the rocks
as the Coast Guard men tossed us lines,
came aboard, and we belonged
to them. ER diagnostics: the hull fitting
for the bilge pump broke off.
Water got in with no way out,
liquid ballast slowly tipping the ship.

In search of the "Big One"
we took a small bite of the sea –
almost more than we could swallow—
or Neptune hooked us,
then threw us back

into the air, no keeper
in his ancient derby.
No limit on mariners, but some days
they put up a fight, spit out the bait
and get away.

GAY HEAD LIGHT

Nothing gay this gray morning.
The salt-sprayed trees
and bushes bend over
like scared school kids,
tested by a towering teacher –
all brick, iron and glaring
glass – missing nothing.

We feel her check on us,
then stare out to sea –
stern but searching
for that last tardy boat
or overdue pilot.
We know that look:
like a hickory stick,
she'll set them straight.

For Todd Follensbee

NORTON POINT

By late August, big tires
have worn deep tracks
in the sand roads and on the beach –
one lane out and one lane back –
even some exit ramps
gouged through the dunes to the bay.
If you get out of the van to walk,
it's like wading through hot snow.

Past the dunes, the point widens
and the tracks spread out,
explore both sides, go where they please.
Sometimes wind-grounded birds
take shelter in them. Sometimes
leaving only footprints
is leaving too much.

HOW TO PROTECT AGAINST SHARKS

Do not swim in water
known to be frequented
by dangerous sharks.

Swimming far from shore
increases shark attacks.

Avoid swimming with an animal
such as a dog or horse.

Look carefully
before jumping or diving
from a boat.

Avoid swimming at dusk or at night
when sharks are searching for food.

Never molest a shark.

Keep an eye toward the open waters
for anything suggestive
of an approaching shark.

From "Handbook for Residents and Visitors
to Greater Pine Island" (Florida).

HALLOWEEN

Why is it scarier on an island?
You can only run so far.
Maybe it's the wind chimes
under the arbor somewhere
that can't be found.
Or the white fraying curtain
waving in the window of the shed
where there is no wind.
Or the dry leaves talking back
to the wind I said wasn't there.

The birds stop feeding and go
where birds go when it's dark.
How could I not know you'd come
looking for me tonight.
Were you the guy I passed
at the side of the road
trying to hitch a ride to someplace?
I know I'm not ready yet
to go in that direction,
and that you won't get out
when my turn comes.

MOTHER AT 85

Trying to make Eagle Scout
at 15, I needed all the merit badges
I could get. Bird Study
should have been a snap.
Mother had been pointing them out
all my life, as she built her list
with a beat-up second-edition Peterson guide.

I ignored her then, of course.
So she walked me down
our ordinary street naming
birds she usually heard first,
like they were the neighbors' children
chirping in their yards.

"The cardinal says, 'chew, chew, chew'
the robin says 'cheeriup'. A Chimney Swift
looks like a flying cigar. Brown Creepers
go up trees, nuthatches wind down."
I found my 30 birds in no time
and kept on counting.

Fifty years later, we sit in the car
by the marsh, windows down,
and she can't hear a thing,
can't spot the White-eyed Vireo yelling,
"Honey bring me a beer quick"
or the witchity-witchity of a Yellowthroat
ten feet away. When I try to point
out a Great Blue Heron on a duck blind

100 yards out, I can tell where she's looking
isn't even close. I tell her

to put down her binoculars and just look
with her eyes, like she used to tell me.
When she gets impatient and says,
"It doesn't matter," I won't let her quit.
"It's straight out from the car," I say,
"You see it now, don't you?
You've got to, it's right there!"

OFFICE VISIT

Doc, thanks for telling me
That odd spot on my back's not cancer,
just some cells aging normally.
"Nothing to worry about,"

you told my wife twenty years ago
when she complained of pain
near her neck so sharp
she couldn't sleep. You called it

"tennis shoulder" and gave her
a steroid shot, let it go,
until an X-ray set you straight,
and revealed her fate – dead

at thirty-nine after four months
of hopeless chemotherapy.
"I blew it," you finally said,
and actually hung your head.

I could have cursed you to Hell,
or sued, but instead decided
to become the curse. So just kept on
coming back for physicals, bad colds.

flu shots, year after year – looking
you in the eye, letting you
shake my hand. Now, I know
you'll never forget her, and never
call something nothing again.

TERMINAL VELOCITY

You died a terrible death;
explosive hemorrhage, pain
molecules cutting down walls
of Demerol, dementia.

Then I have to listen
to a priest say it was all
because of free will:
we choose not to fund research.

He can't see
we're just not that smart.
Only a few of us
can even try to cure cancer.

Anyone can get it,
and leave behind a hole
so deep it swallows hymns
of hope without an echo.

(Insert uplifting stanza here.)

FLOTSAM

Notes in bottles often
reach the shore too soon.
Now, like driftwood, this coffin,
cast up at our feet.
Like toadstools or autumn
Goldenrod, he sprang up
from nothing – did little good
or harm to anyone. Hurry,
say some words,
dribble dirt on a cross,
and drown him deep
in brown waves of earth.

VOLCANES DE COLIMA

We are halfway up the cone
we hope stays inactive, balance
on the very edge of the dirt road
while pick-ups roar past,
beds crowded with kids
wrapped in blankets, waving,
happy to be going all the way
up to play in the only snow
they've ever seen.

Last week, a van with six
fell all the way back down
to bare rock, right
where we are huddled
together trying to see the flash
of an Amethyst Hummingbird
in the late sun.
If their spirits got wings,
come out to catch some rays,
we'll get a glimpse and smile.

-Colima, Mexico

STOPOVER

This flat field, hayed in September,
looks empty –
short green grass just
getting going –
but there are birds feeding
all around us, almost hidden.

Hardy seafarers, with tough names –
plovers, pec's, dow's, turnstones –
getting built up for the long flight south.

Then all at once, the flock is up, spinning
around us, whirlwind of wings
that flash white then go dark
as the birds veer away, then back,
then almost touch down at our feet.

There's food. They must want
to stay. But the gyres get wider,
bird profiles diminish.
"Lift us," we say without speaking,
"lift us up and take us along."

NAVIGATOR

At 4 a.m., the Southern Cross
hangs like kite moored above the lights
of Panama City, still bright from Carnival –
Mardi Gras – that shut down the town
for four days. Two thousand years or so

ago, with sun, wind and birds, Crux helped
steer Polynesian canoes east from Asian islands
to Hawaii and Samoa. Far to our south,
sailors didn't care that we can also see

Big Bear chasing Little Bear in circles
north, just above the trees. No bears
down here, but African slaves saw
the drinking gourd, the big dipper,

and sang about how you could follow it
until it rose up, almost overhead,
and then you were free.

GARBAGE COLLECTION — SOUTH PHILLY

The sky is clear
    but irrelevant.
However, the row houses notice,
    are self-conscious.
Hear them come
    the three!
In army surplus
like leopard skins,
they beat
    the trashcans
    war drums
    down Wolf Street.

THE CHAIR

Walking alone on the foggy beach
I find a plastic chair
on its side at the high tide line,
left behind or washed in
last night. I tip it up
and sit a minute counting waves.

Tiny figures of beachcombers
to the north and south –
no one even approaching.
I could just leave
my wallet and keys on the chair
and disappear into the mist,

from this version of my life.
Farfetched? Last night
I met a broke young captain
who would take me anywhere
I'd pay to go, so he wouldn't
have to store his boat
and get a real job.

Of course, I got up and went back
to the rented house, the wife,
the kids, all waking with fresh demands.
Or that's what you think
I did, instead of submitting
this poem with a borrowed name
(thanks Warren) from far away
and then moving on.

SEVENTH DECADE

After wine, talk of work,
and catching up,
I went to lie down.
It was still light out –
close to the solstice.

When I reached to close
the curtains, I came face-to-face
with a new hibiscus blossom.
It said, "Don't you want
to come live with me?"

SYNCHRONICITY

100 million light years from here
two galaxies collide

10 million light years from here
two solar systems unite

8 light years from here
two stars fuse

Here, two drops of melt water
hit the lake a foot apart

send out concentric waves
that orbit the entry points
collide or unite
reinforce or cancel

The lake is so still
this evening isn't it?

POEM

The walking cat carefully
balances on its shadow.
Andromeda wheels on a pin.
But I must turn on thoughts
and never know where
I will face
at dawn.

ABOUT THE AUTHOR

WARREN WOESSNER is the Senior Editor of *Abraxas,* which he co-founded in 1968. He also was a co-founder of WORT-FM in Madison, WI. Five collections of his poetry have been published, most recently *Clear All the Rest of the Way* (The Backwaters Press). He has received Fellowships in Poetry from the NEA, the Wisconsin Arts Board and the McKnight Foundation. Warren holds a Ph.D. in chemistry and a J.D. from the University of Wisconsin, Madison. He co-founded Schwegman, Lundberg & Woessner in 1993, where he works as a biotechnology patent attorney.

Woessner's poetry has been widely published and anthologized, including *Poetry, Poetry Northwest, The Nation, 5 AM, Nimrod, Midwest Quarterly* and *The Beloit Pooetry Journal.* He won the Minnesota Voices Competition sponsored by New Rivers Press in 1986.

ABOUT THE COVER PHOTOGRAPHER

I was raised in Kent, CT, on an old non-working farm straddling the New York-Connecticut border line, about a quarter mile from the Housatonic River. My education after elementary school included a year in Lausanne, four years at Hotchkiss, and a History of Art degree from Yale, with my summers spent on Martha's Vineyard every year. Soon after marrying in 1970, I built my first house in West Tisbury, MA, and a cabin in Nova Scotia soon after. You might encounter me birding on the Vineyard any day, any season, camera in hand.
http://lannymcdowellart.com